OVERTOUN BRIDGE

This series features unsolved mysteries, urban legends, and other curious stories. Each creepy, shocking, or befuddling book focuses on what people believe and hear. True or not? That's for you to decide!

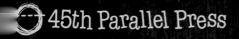
45th Parallel Press

Published in the United States of America by Cherry Lake Publishing
Ann Arbor, Michigan
www.cherrylakepublishing.com

Author: Virginia Loh-Hagan
Reading Adviser: Marla Conn MS, Ed., Literacy specialist, Read-Ability, Inc.
Book Designer: Felicia Macheske

Photo Credits: © kovop58/Shutterstock.com, cover; © Marjan Apostolovic/Shutterstock.com, 5; © Jaaebaby Q Taro/
Shutterstock.com, 7; © Twinsterphoto/Shutterstock.com, 8; © TreasureGalore/Shutterstock.com, 11; © Lairich Rig/
CC BY-SA 2.0, via www.geograph.org.uk, 13, 17; © claupad/Shutterstock.com, 14; © Christin Lola/Shutterstock.com, 18;
© Evdoha_spb/Shutterstock.com, 21; © Joseph Sohm/Shutterstock.com, 22; © arhendrix/Shutterstock.com, 25;
© Alexey Stiop/Shutterstock.com, 26; © Sandra Standbridge/Shutterstock.com, 29

Graphic Elements Throughout: © iofoto/Shutterstock.com; © COLCU/Shutterstock.com; © spacedrone808/
Shutterstock.com; © rf.vector.stock/Shutterstock.com; © donatas1205/Shutterstock.com; © cluckva/Shutterstock.
com; © Eky Studio/Shutterstock.com

45th Parallel Press is an imprint of Cherry Lake Publishing.

Library of Congress Cataloging-in-Publication Data has been filed and is available at catalog.loc.gov

Cherry Lake Publishing would like to acknowledge the work of The Partnership for 21st Century Skills.
Please visit *www.p21.org* for more information.

Printed in the United States of America
Corporate Graphics

TABLE OF CONTENTS

Chapter One

THE BRIDGE OF DEATH

Who is Kevin Moy? Who is Ben? Who is Hendrix?

Kevin Moy was at Overtoun Bridge. He had a baby son. His son was 2 weeks old. Moy threw his son over the bridge. His son died. Moy believed his son was the devil.

He tried to jump off the bridge. He tried to kill himself. But his wife pulled him back. She saved his life. This happened in October 1994. Moy was 32 years old.

The cops arrested him. Moy told the cops he was trying to save the world. He had to kill his baby to do this. He went to court. The jury found him not guilty. They found him to be **insane**. Insane means being crazy.

Rumor is that Moy was on drugs.

CONSIDER THE
EVIDENCE

Alice Trevorrow is a dog owner. Her son is Thomas. Her dog is Cassie. Cassie is a 3 year old springer spaniel. Alice, Thomas, and Cassie walked across the Overtoun Bridge. Cassie looked left. Then, she suddenly jumped off. She made a whining sound. She jumped 50 feet (15 meters). Alice and Thomas were scared. They looked over the bridge. They were shocked. Cassie survived. She struggled to her feet. She pulled a muscle in her back leg. She didn't have any broken bones. Alice said, "My heart just dropped. I have no idea how she survived. The bridge is so high. I was almost certain that she had died.... It is a complete miracle."

The Moy baby was the only human death at the bridge. But many dogs have died there.

Donna Cooper walked across the bridge. She was with her dog, husband, and son. Her dog was named Ben. Ben was a collie. He jumped off the bridge. He did this without warning. He landed on the rocks. He broke his paw. He broke his back. He broke his jaw. Cooper took Ben to the **vet**. Vets are animal doctors. The vet said Ben was in too much pain to live. They had to put him down. This happened in 1995.

Sometimes pets get injuries they can't recover from.

People love their dogs. They don't want them to get hurt.

Kenneth Meikle knows how the Cooper family feels. He almost lost his dog, Hendrix, at the bridge. Hendrix is a golden retriever. Meikle said, "I was out walking with my partner and children when suddenly, the dog just jumped. My daughter screamed."

Meikle ran down to Hendrix. He picked her up. He carried her to safety. He said, "As I did so, her hair started to fall out." Hendrix was in shock. She shook all night long.

Hendrix survived. She's one of the few dogs to do so. Meikle said, "We were lucky because she landed on a **moss** bed, which broke her fall." Moss is soft grass.

Chapter Two

TAKING A LEAP

Where is Overtoun Bridge? What happens at Overtoun Bridge?

Overtoun Bridge is in Scotland. It was completed in 1895. It was designed by H. E. Milner. It's made of stone. It spans a **gorge**. Gorges are deep, narrow valleys. They have steep rocky sides. They have streams flowing through them.

It's a famous bridge. Something about it lures dogs to jump. It's called the "dog **suicide** bridge." Suicide is the act of killing oneself. There's something odd about the bridge. Dogs jump off it. They fall 50 feet (15 m). They land on the sharp rocks below. Many are killed. This has been happening since the 1950s.

The bridge is located near Dumbarton in Scotland.

SPOTLIGHT
BIOGRAPHY

Judy Smith-Hill lives in Canada. She was a dog groomer. She retired from that job. But she still cares for dogs. She fostered dogs. Then, she started her own rescue group. She did this in August 2012. She focused on senior dogs. She's in charge of the Before the Bridge Senior K9 Rescue. These senior dogs are over 8 years old. Smith said, "There's a need for senior dogs to have a place to go rather than be euthanized." Euthanized means to be killed. Dogs that don't get adopted get killed. Most people want to adopt puppies. Senior dogs get left behind. Smith has found homes for more than 250 dogs. She said, "I'm just a senior rescuing seniors."

About one dog per year jumps off the bridge. About 50 dogs in the last 50 years have died. Hundreds of dogs have jumped and lived. Some dogs survive. But they go back. They jump again. It's odd.

Dogs always jump off the same side. They jump from the same spot. They jump from between the last two **parapets** on the right-hand side. Parapets are low walls. They're along the edge of the bridge. They're like safety barriers.

Dogs always jump in the same weather. They jump on clear, sunny days.

There's nothing special about the way Overtoun Bridge is built.

For some reason, dogs react negatively on the bridge.

Only dogs jump. No other animals feel the need to jump. And only specific dog **breeds** jump. Breeds are dog types. Only dogs with long **snouts** jump. A snout is the mouth and nose area. These breeds include collies and retrievers.

No one knows why this is happening. Dog owners are upset about this. The Scottish Society for the Prevention of Cruelty to Animals (SSPCA) investigated. They didn't find anything. Dorren Graham works for the SSPCA. Graham calls Overtoun Bridge a "**heartbreaking** mystery." Heartbreaking means sad. No one wants dogs to die or get hurt.

Chapter Three

A HAUNTED HISTORY

Why was Overtoun Bridge built? Who haunts the area?

Overtoun Bridge is named for Lord Overtoun's family. Overtoun House is a 19th-century country house. It's on a hill. It overlooks a river.

John White was a retired lawyer. He bought the Overtoun lands. He did this in 1859. He also bought lands close to his house. He needed a road and bridge to connect the old and new lands. The eastern and western sides were split by a waterfall. White had Overtoun Bridge built. Overtoun Burn is the name of the stream that runs under it.

Overtoun Bridge has three arches.

Lady Overtoun may want loyal ghost dogs.

White became Baron Overtoun in 1893. He died in 1908. He didn't have any children. His wife was Lady Overtoun. She lived in the house until 1931. After her death, Overtoun House was given to the town. The house was used as a hospital. It was used as a lab. It was used as a religious center.

Many people think the house is haunted. They think Lady Overtoun is a ghost. People have reported seeing her ghost. They mainly see her ghost in the house. But some people think that her ghost also haunts the bridge. Some people think her ghost lures dogs.

REAL-WORLD
CONNECTION

The T. Tyler Potterfield Bridge is in Richmond, Virginia. It has metal strips. There are small gaps between the strips. These strips hurt dogs. Dogs get their toenails stuck. This splits their nails. It causes pain. It causes bleeding. Greg Velzy has two dogs. He said, "Imagine your fingernail getting ripped off. . . . A dog doesn't know to stop pulling. They just keep yanking and yanking to stop the pain. And it just makes it worse." Scott Adams owns two dogs. His dogs' nails broke. Adams said, "As an owner, you feel terrible that this happens." The bridge has had many complaints. Dog owners are warning others.

Chapter Four

THE THIN PLACE

What is the thin place? How does this affect dogs? What's another explanation?

Scottish people believe in **Celtic** stories. Celtic refers to ancient Scottish people.

Overtoun Bridge is thought to be a "thin place" as believed by the Celtic people. This is an area where heaven and Earth are at their closest. It's the barrier between the land of the living and the land of the dead. The barrier is thin here. This means it's weak. Ghosts can cross over to Earth. Living things can cross over to death.

Dogs are more sensitive than humans. They can feel the thin place. They may be able to see ghosts. This may make them act strangely. It could be why they jump.

Being close to the thin place may spook dogs.

Dogs can see things humans can't. Some people think dogs can see the thin place. Most humans can't see it. But Kevin Moy may have seen it. Some people think that's why he went insane.

Dogs can hear things humans can't. Some people blame a naval base for the dogs' jumping. Her Majesty's Naval Base in Faslane is nearby. People believe secret naval messages make a special sound. Only dogs can hear this sound. This sound makes them jump.

The nearby phone lines could also make sounds that might confuse dogs.

INVESTIGATION TIPS

- Talk to someone who's been to Overtoun Bridge. Ask them if they saw anything strange.

- Visit Overtoun Bridge. Find out all you can about its history. Read newspapers. Talk to town historians. Talk to people who live close by.

- Check out the area in daylight. Become familiar with the area. Look for dangerous things that you won't be able to see in the dark.

- See if there are ghosts at Overtoun Bridge. Go ghost hunting. The best time to see ghosts is from 9:00 p.m. to 6:00 a.m. Don't go alone. Be safe.

Chapter Five

DOGS BEING DOGS

What are some scientific explanations for Overtoun Bridge?

Joyce Stewart is an expert. She studies animal behaviors. She works for the SSPCA. She said, "Dogs are very able to **gauge** the heights and depths they can safely jump. [Gauge means to figure out.] I have never heard of a dog committing suicide. Often if they know they are going to die, they might go into hiding, but I have never heard of them actually taking their own lives."

Most experts agree with Stewart. They don't think dogs are killing themselves. Dogs can get sad. But they're not suicidal.

Dogs can miss people, look tired, and stop eating when sad.

Dogs can sense their owners' feelings from far away.

Dogs can sense the feelings of their owners. There are many studies that prove this. There's no longer a great need for working dogs. Humans get dogs for fun. Dogs are part of the family. Experts think humans are transferring their feelings to dogs. This makes dogs feel responsible for their owners.

Some people think dogs that jump off Overtoun Bridge are sensing their owners feelings. These dogs are picking up their owners' sad thoughts. They act on their owners' moods. The town around Overtoun is a sad place. The town is poor. People are losing their jobs. This may cause people to be sad.

EXPLAINED BY SCIENCE

Dogs came from wolves. They've been separated from wolves for more than 100,000 years. Wolves that became dogs bonded with humans. Humans cared for them. This is how dogs survived. Dogs were the first tamed animals. Dogs helped early humans survive. A scientist said, "Humans domesticated dogs, and dogs domesticated humans." Domesticated means to tame. Humans relied on dogs. Dogs heard dangers. They sniffed for food. As a result, humans' smelling and hearing skills weakened.

David Sexton is an animal **habitat** expert. Habitats are homes. Dr. David Sands is a dog psychologist. The two men investigated Overtoun Bridge. They studied sights, smells, and sounds. They found **mink** under the bridge.

Dogs like the smell of mink. Male minks have strong pee. They mark their space. They pee all over. Their smells are strongest on sunny, dry days. Rainy days reduce the smell.

Dogs only see stone on the bridge. They focus on smell. Their other senses are dulled. They don't see the long drop until it's too late.

Real or not? It doesn't matter. The Overtoun Bridge lives in people's imaginations. It also lives in dogs' imaginations.

Mice and squirrels also live under the bridge.

DID YOU KNOW?

There's a warning sign on Overtoun Bridge. It reads, "Dangerous bridge—Keep your dog on a lead." Lead is another word for leash.

Dogs with longer snouts may have a harder time seeing objects in front of them. Their snouts block their field of vision.

Humans see 180 degrees around them. Dogs can see 240 degrees around them. They see more while looking straight ahead.

Anthrozoology is a new field of study. It's the study of human and animal interactions.

Many people believe in the mink theory. But some don't. John Joyce is a local hunter. He has lived in the area for over 50 years. He said, "There are no mink around here. I can tell you that with absolute certainty."

Mary Armour is a psychic. Psychics say they can see the future. She took her dog to Overtoun Bridge. She said, "Animals are hypersensitive to the spirit-world. But I didn't feel any adverse energy." But her dog did pull a little to the right.

Minks came to Scotland in the 1920s. But they started to overbreed in the 1950s. This is when dogs started jumping.

CONSIDER THIS!

Take a Position: **Reread chapters 4 and 5. There are several explanations for the mystery of Overtoun Bridge. Which explanation makes the most sense to you? Why do you think so? Argue your point with reasons and evidence.**

Say What? **Scotland has a lot of haunted places. An example is the Black Mausoleum. (Read the 45th Parallel Press book *MacKenzie Poltergeist*.) How would you compare Overtoun Bridge to Scotland's other scary places?**

Think About It! **Gephyrophobia is a fear of bridges. Some people are really scared of crossing bridges. They may be scared of small spaces and heights. How do you feel about bridges?**

LEARN MORE

- Omoth, Tyler. *Handbook to Stonehenge, the Bermuda Triangle, and Other Mysterious Locations*. North Mankato, MN: Capstone Press, 2017.

- *Overtoun: Uncovering the Mystery*, documentary film (MFN Productions, 2014).

GLOSSARY

breeds (BREEDZ) types of dogs

Celtic (KEL-tik) of the Celts, the ancient people of Scotland

gauge (GAYJ) to figure out

gorge (GORJ) a deep, narrow valley with steep rocky sides and streams flowing through

habitat (HAB-ih-tat) home

heartbreaking (HAHRT-brayk-ing) sad

insane (in-SANE) crazy

mink (MINGK) a small animal with soft dark brown fur, often raised for its fur

moss (MAWS) soft grass

parapets (PAR-uh-pets) low walls along the edges of a bridge, safety barriers

snouts (SNOUTS) nose and mouth areas, long noses of a dog

suicide (SOO-ih-side) the act of killing oneself

vet (VET) veterinarian, animal doctor

INDEX

ABOUT THE AUTHOR

Dr. Virginia Loh-Hagan is an author, university professor, former classroom teacher, and curriculum designer. She lives in San Diego with her very tall husband and very naughty dogs. She loves her dogs so much. To learn more about her, visit www.virginialoh.com.